THE MEDITERRANEAN DIET FOR BEGINNERS

A Practical Strategy Guide
Featuring Simple Rules for Weight Loss,
and a 14 Day Diet Meal Plan

PETER BRAGG

Legal & Disclaimer

The information contained in this book and its contents is not designed to replace or take the place of any form of medical or professional advice; and is not meant to replace the need for independent medical, financial, legal or other professional advice or services, as may be required. The content and information in this book has been provided for educational and entertainment purposes only.

The content and information contained in this book has been compiled from sources deemed reliable, and it is accurate to the best of the Author's knowledge, information, and belief. However, the Author cannot guarantee its accuracy and validity and cannot be held liable for any errors and/or omissions. Further, changes are periodically made to this book as and when needed. Where appropriate and/or necessary, you must consult a professional (including but not limited to your doctor, attorney, financial advisor or such other professional advisor) before using any of the suggested remedies, techniques, or information in this book.

Upon using the contents and information contained in this book, you agree to hold harmless the Author from and against any damages, costs, and expenses, including any legal fees potentially resulting from the application of any of the information provided by this book. This disclaimer applies to any loss, damages or injury caused by the use and application, whether directly or indirectly, of any advice or information presented, whether for breach of contract, tort, negligence, personal injury, criminal intent, or under any other cause of action.

You agree to accept all risks of using the information presented in this book.

You agree that by continuing to read this book, where appropriate and/or necessary, you shall consult a professional (including but not limited to your doctor, attorney, or financial advisor or such other advisor as needed) before using any of the suggested remedies, techniques, or information in this book.

Table of Contents

Description

Have you been looking at those models in magazines and wishing you could fit in those clothes and look that good? Tell me honestly, how many times have you purchased a pair of pants that are a few inches smaller than your waistline, thinking you may fit into those once you lose some weight? If you are guilty of doing something like this, you are definitely not alone. For starters, stop trying to force your body to take on an unnatural shape. Don't try to slim down just because you want to look like those models on the billboards. And for heaven's sake don't starve yourself in order to shed that stubborn fat. You will only end up disappointing yourself with the lack of energy and sagging skin these crash diets cause. While it's certainly not right to hate your body if you are obese, you can take up a diet that doesn't starve you, and offers ample nutrition while leaving you feeling energized. If you have been stressed with your weight issues for a while, it's time to take up the Mediterranean diet.

Many people have dreamt about a diet without a strictly written menu for every day. There is need to focus on a well-balanced diet that offers tasty and diverse food while at the same time boosts your health and keeps your fit. Believe it or not, the Mediterranean diet meets all these parameters and is considered to be one of the healthiest dietary patterns in the world.

Additionally, it serves as a general set of guidelines to nudge you into a healthier, happier lifestyle rather than listing off a series of foods that cannot be eaten.

You can use this book as a guide to help you get started on your new lifestyle should you be unfamiliar with the Mediterranean diet. You will be able to open up a whole new world for yourself and understand more details about the Mediterranean diet, such as the benefits, the tips and rules you need to follow, the recipes, and a 14-day plan. Why not try the recipes in this book, there is nothing to lose—except for some bad habits that is! Enjoy the journey.

Introduction

There are so many things that I love about the Mediterranean diet. It includes whole natural foods, is easy to adapt to your lifestyle and in short....is the healthiest diet in the world. When you eat the Mediterranean way you nourish your body in a balanced way that allows it to function at its best.

When eating well tastes like a yearlong vacation, it's easy and exciting to indulge in. It is highly likely that after reading this book, you will see a plate of healthy, colorful, and delicious food according to the best principles of the Mediterranean diet on your dinner table.

That being said, it is important before beginning any diet you consult your doctor or physician. The Mediterranean diet isn't right for everyone. I'll go over this more in a later chapter but you should always ask your physician if this diet is correct for your set of circumstances. The goal here is to get healthier. I'm not a physician, I'm just a person who believes in the transformative power of the Mediterranean diet. I've seen the positive changes it can make in a person's life and I want to see that same positive change for all of you.

If you're already familiar with the Mediterranean diet, I hope you enjoy all the recipes I've included. They should keep you eating well for the foreseeable future. I'm excited to begin. Let's get started!

What is the Mediterranean Diet

The Mediterranean diet is more than a diet. It is a lifestyle. It's a way of eating in order to live a full and healthy life. When following this way of eating you'll not only lose weight but you'll also strengthen your heart and provide your body with all the proper nutrients necessary to live a long and productive life. People following the Mediterranean diet have been linked to a lower risk of Alzheimer's disease and cancer, better overall cardiovascular health, and an extended lifespan. The building blocks that comprise a Mediterranean diet are foods rich in healthy oils, low in saturated fat, and filled with vegetables and fresh fruits.

The Mediterranean diet focuses on typical foods and recipes you'd find in Mediterranean-style cooking. Here's what goes into the Mediterranean diet. This diet includes consuming lots of vegetables and grains, fruits, rice, and pasta while limiting fats, replacing salt with herbs and spices, and eating fish and poultry instead of red meat. The Mediterranean diet does not contain a lot of red meat. Nuts are a part of a healthy part of this diet. However, one should limit themselves to a handful or so a day. Nuts have a high amount of fat but a high percentage of the fat isn't saturated. Nuts are also high in calories so carefully monitor the amount you eat. You'll want to avoid salted nuts and honey roasted or candied nuts.

It may ven include a glass of red wine per day, and regular physical activities to fully maximize the remarkable health benefits. The Mediterranean diet reflects various eating habits of the countries near the Mediterranean Sea, mainly Southern Italy, Greece, Morocco, France, and Spain. Due to their unique locality, the climate supports fresh fruits, vegetables, and some of the world's best seafood.

This diet isn't focused on limiting your total consumption of fat, instead, it focuses on making smarter choices about the kinds of fat you consume. This diet discourages people from eating trans-fats and saturated fats, both of which have been linked to heart disease.

Grains used in the Mediterranean diet are preferably whole grain, which generally contain very little in the way of unhealthy trans-fat. Bread is an important part of the Mediterranean lifestyle, however bread should not to be covered in margarine or butter. Instead, the bread is eaten either dipped in olive oil or eaten plain. This cuts down significantly on a number of trans and saturated fats normally associated with eating bread.

Wine plays a large role in the Mediterranean diet. A glass of wine is normally included with each evening meal. This means 5 ounces or less of wine for anyone over the age of 65 and for people under 65 no more than 10 ounces daily. If you have any history of alcohol dependency or abuse I suggest refraining altogether from consuming alcohol as part of your diet. The same goes if you already have liver or heart disease.

Olive oil is the primary source of fat in this type of diet. It actually provides monounsaturated fat, which is the kind of fat that helps reduce the levels of LDL cholesterol when utilized instead of trans or saturated fats. The "Extra virgin" and "virgin" olive oils are considered to have undergone the least processing. They also happen to contain the largest levels of protective plant compounds responsible for providing antioxidant effects.

What is LDL?

Cholesterol is a compound belonging to the sterol or steroid alcohol subgroup of organic molecules. It is classified as a waxy steroid of fat. It is an essential component of cellular membranes and a precursor to the production of fat-soluble vitamins, such as vitamin D.

There are two main types of cholesterol; HDL (high-density lipoproteins) and LDL (low-density lipoproteins). Though this is not entirely accurate. HDL and LDL are lipoproteins. They are the transport mechanisms for cholesterol particles. They are composed of proteins and fats.

LDL particles transport cholesterols from the liver to the cells of the body.

HDLs collect any that is found in the tissues or produced by other organs and carry it back to the liver for reprocessing.

This is why HDLs are sometimes referred to as "good" cholesterol, because they pick up any that is dropped in the bloodstream before it can adhere to the walls of the arteries. LDL is known as the bad cholesterol.

Although it is essential for life, large amounts of cholesterol in the bloodstream may increase a person's risk of heart disease, mainly atherosclerosis. This is why balance in HDL/LDL particles is so important and an imbalance can be dangerous.

Highlight on Trans-fats

Trans-fats are listed as hydrogenated or partially hydrogenated oils. The oils may be soy, canola or simply listed as partially hydrogenated "vegetable" il. This kind of fat is the worst kind you can possibly eat. According to the Mayo Clinic, trans-fats raise LDL levels and lowers HDL levels. It is a man-made fat that is found in baked goods and other packaged foods. In addition to causing HDL/LDL imbalance, it raises total blood triglycerides (fats that normally circulate in the bloodstream) and promotes plaque buildup on arterial walls. Like obesity, trans-fat also contributes to chronic inflammation.

Another major component of the Mediterranean diet is fatty fish.

This includes lake trout, salmon, sardines, herring, mackerel, and albacore tuna. They have plenty of omega-3 fatty acids.

This type of fatty acid helps to decrease blood clotting and lower our triglyceride levels. High triglyceride levels (more than 150 mg/dL) can cause heart diseases. Omega-3 fatty acids are also associated with helping to moderate blood pressure, decrease the risk of sudden heart attack, and improve the overall health of our blood vessels.

I often get asked how many times per week can eat certain types of foods. Well, on the Mediterranean diet you can enjoy foods like yogurt, cheese, vegetables, whole grains, beans, and fruits daily. However, fish, eggs, and meat should only be served once or twice each week. You'll find that this is easier to do than you tink, especially after a couple of weeks once you've readjusted to your new way of eating. I have a ton of delicious recipes you can try out in later chapters.

The Mediterranean diet is 35 to 40 percent fat. However, the diet is focused primarily on healthy fats. Though higher in calories, fats make your food taste better and your meals feel more satisfying. You will eat a little less but enjoy your food significantly more.

I often hear people ask if they'll always feel hungry when following this diet. The answer to that is a resounding "NO". Since the Mediterranean diet places emphasis on high fiber nutrients rich foods like vegetables, beans, fresh fruits, legumes, and whole grains you'll never have the intense hunger pangs associated with so many other diets on the market.

You may be eating less each day but your stomach won't feel that way.

The Mediterranean lifestyle itself plays a large role in supporting your diet plan. You'll want to get plenty of exercises but still carve out time to have long leisurely meals with your family and friends.

The good thing about the Mediterranean diet is that it doesn't require you to buy any special kind of foods. No money will be wasted on buying foods that are labeled as being low-fat or diet. Though there are exceptions, a Mediterranean diet consists of less processed, natural food. The more natural foods you incorporate into your daily diet the healthier you'll be. Being on a Mediterranean diet requires commitment. You'll be spending more time preparing your meals in your kitchen. Since you're eating natural foods, they won't already be processed and ready to go. I suggest brushing up on your cooking skills or taking a class if you have no skills to speak of. I love to cook so this wasn't too big of a change for me. However, I have friends who had zero skills in the kitchen and they found this to be a daunting challenge at first.

I plan out my weekly meals on Friday nights. Each Saturday I shop for all my food and then I prepare the majority of my meals in advance on Sunday. Having a schedule and system in place makes the entire process go much smoother. It also ensures I always have a healthy meal on hand in case I'm feeling unmotivated to cook for myself at certain times of the week.

As with most diets, it's also very important to stay well hydrated when on this diet. Drink 64 oz. or 8 glasses of water on a daily basis. If you ever feel like you're getting a headache or a muscle cramp, you may just need some water.

I also suggest keeping a daily log of your meals. I go over what I use in the resources section. Keeping track of what you're eating is a good tool to help keep you motivated and on point. It will be a good way to identify the things throw you off course. For instance, when I first started I noticed my food intake was terrible on Sunday. This was because for much of the year I would spend Sunday afternoons watching football with friends while eating and drinking non-stop. Once I saw what I was consuming compared to the rest of my week, I knew what changes I needed to make to keep me on track.

Don't forget to check with your physician before starting on this diet. I know it sounds like a giant hassle but you should always determine a proper course of action with a trained professional before getting started.

Major Features of a Mediterranean Diet:

1. The primary source of your fat in this diet is olive oil.
2. Dinner often includes a glass of red wine.
3. Vegetables and seasonal fresh fruits are a major part of every meal.
4. Whole grain pasta and bread are served without any type of apology,

5. Meat is consumed in smaller portions and red meat is primarily avoided altogether.

6. Popular flavors include garlic, basil, oregano, lemon, rosemary, and mint.

Benefits of the Mediterranean Diet

Many studies prove the many advantages of the Mediterranean Diet. However, even if you don't look at the studies, the Mediterranean people serve as first-hand proof of the benefits of this wonderful diet. Here are a number of benefits from going on the Mediterranean Diet.

Long and Healthy Life

The Mediterranean cuisine is often referred to as the healthiest cuisine in the world and the diet doesn't stray too far away. Being based mostly on fresh vegetables and fruits, healthy oils and whole grains, as well as lean meat and seafood, it's not hard to see why this diet is considered to be healthy. Mix with a glass of red wine and you've got yourself a fun, easy going diet.

Your Heart Will Thank You

Scientific evidence easily connects good heart health with certain foods, mainly vegetables, fruits, olive oil, and nuts. The Mediterranean diet has it all!

The Mediterranean diet is all about highlighting healthy fats. Instead of using the usual cooking oil, the diet uses olive oil which contains healthy fat that is good for the heart. With that said, the Mediterranean Diet can help decrease your risk of heart failure. A Mediterranean diet consists of food with monounsaturated fats like olive oil rather than saturated fats like butter.

The Mediterranean diet naturally includes most of the key diet changes that would keep your heart in tip-top shape

Shed Some Unwanted Weight

Although the main focus of this diet is not weight loss, it will surely help with it if that's what you're looking for. Just look at it from this point of view: fresh, clean food combined with whole grains, good fats, less sugar and plenty of liquids coupled with copious amounts of exercise. By transitioning to healthy foods and a healthy lifestyle, you'll shed pounds without causing drastic imbalances in your body. Also, it is known that plant-based diets like the Mediterranean diet are really helpful in losing weight. The mere fact that you stopped eating junk food and processed food with sugar and unhealthy fats is already a very good start to weight loss!

Controls Diabetes

Because it focuses on fresh ingredients and it packs plenty of vitamins, antioxidants, and minerals, this diet is a great way to keep your diabetes under control. This lifestyle controls excess insulin, which in turn lowers our blood sugar levels.

Regulating blood sugar levels is vastly important to living a healthier lifestyle. There is need of balancing a lot of whole foods into this plan to find quality sources of protein and consume carbs that are low in sugar. That makes the body burn fat much more efficiently, and you will have more energy as a result.

In short, a natural diet with fresh produce is a natural combater of diabetes.

It is Affordable

The Mediterranean diet is accessible even if you're on a budget. Legumes, vegetables, fruits, herbs, whole grains and olive oil are not as expensive as they sound, but they offer so much versatility in the kitchen.

Boost Brain Power

The Mediterranean Diet can also counteract the brain's poor ability to perform. Choosing this lifestyle will actually help you preserve your memory, leading to an overall increase in your cognitive health.

Normally cognitive disorders are caused by a scenario where your brain is unable to get sufficient amount of dopamine.

Dopamine is a compound or chemical present in the brain responsible for passing information from one neuron to the other. It is responsible for thought processing, mood regulation and proper body movements.

The ability of the Mediterranean diet to help boost your cognitive health is normally linked to the combination of its anti-inflammatory fruits and vegetables, its healthy fats and nuts. These foods normally battle cognitive decline that is caused by age. But how do these foods do it?

These foods normally deal with elements that cause impaired brain function like inflammation, free radicals and exposure to toxicity.

Fatty fish, nuts and olive oils all contain omega 3 fatty acids that usually help reduce the level of inflammation in your body. Such vegetables like spinach, kale and broccoli that are dark green contain vitamin E, which is known to protect your body from an anti-inflammatory molecule known as cytokines.

Vegetables like spinach, broccoli and fruits like raspberries, cherries and watermelon all have antioxidants that neutralize free radicals that affect your brain. The Mediterranean diet also tends to focus on monounsaturated fats which come from oils like olive oil. The oils and the fatty acids that you get from omega 3 (from fish) combine to keep your arteries unblocked.

That automatically increases the health of your brain and reduces your risk of getting diseases like Alzheimer disease and dementia.

Encourage Relaxation

The Mediterranean Diet surprisingly enough, can encourage relaxation. The diet can lower your levels of insulin and make you feel at ease. High blood sugar can cause you to be hyperactive and later crash; but eating balanced meals with lots of whole grains, fruits, veggies, etc. actually helps stabilize blood sugar, allowing you to relax and rest. Since a major component of this lifestyle is eating with the family at the dinner table, relaxation is maximized. With a home-cooked meal in your comfort zone, relaxation will be evident with this diet.

Enhance Your Mood

The diet can help you to be positive, even when things aren't going your way. Healthy living does that. When you have eaten enough food to fuel you with lots of nutrients, your body notices. Fulfillment and productivity enhance your mood. For one, applying the diet correctly will make you feel like you're doing something good for yourself, and thus enhances your overall mood.

Improve Skin Condition

Fish have Omega-3 fatty acids. They strengthen the skin membrane, and make it more elastic and firmer. Olive oil, red wine, and tomatoes contain a lot of antioxidants to protect against skin damage brought about by chemical reactions and prolonged sun exposure.

Disadvantages of the Mediterranean Diet:

While the Mediterranean Diet clearly has incredible benefits and has proven to be really effective in keeping terminal illnesses at bay for generations, it's worth noting that it also has some disadvantages. After all, a perfect diet does not exist.

1. **Not Specific.** The Mediterranean works its magic and all, but it's the spell you need to know to make it work. However, the diet really does not have a specific "spell". For instance, the foods in the diet vary as the different Mediterranean countries and cities use different varieties of it. For example, Greece and Italy have different preferred food on their tables. There are no official and exact names of certain foods to eat; it only shows generic terminology like fruits, vegetables, fish, and more. Additionally, it doesn't show how much to eat so it could get quite tricky to know exactly if you've overeaten or if you did not follow the diet at all.

2. **Not for some people**. Some of the foods included in the diet have gluten and there are people who are sensitive to gluten. People with peanut and seafood allergies would also find it hard to follow the Mediterranean Diet as nuts and fish are a major part of the diet. Also, as the diet could require planning the menu and preparing the dishes at home, those who don't have time to cook will find it challenging to follow this.

3. **Not an overnighter**. The Mediterranean people are as healthy as they are because their diet is traditional; they have been on it their whole lives. So if you expect results after one day, reign in those unrealistic expectations. In order to get positive, long-lasting results, don't let the Mediterranean Diet be just a passing diet craze. You have to breathe it, live it, and eat it; just like real Mediterranean people.

Being Keen on a Mediterranean Diet

If you don't manage your diet closely you may suffer from these common side effect. Luckily, there are easy ways to prevent these from becoming an issue.

1. You may start to gain weight if you don't monitor the amount of nuts and olive oil you consume. These are very high in fat so you need to keep an eye on how much you're having each day.
2. You could have some calcium loss from eating less dairy. If it happens to you, ask your doctor if you should begin taking some form of calcium supplement.
3. You may find that your iron levels are low. Be sure to eat more foods rich in vitamin C or iron.

If you have any issues with alcohol, I suggest abstaining from incorporating it into your diet. The idea is to get healthy not endanger yourself further. As you can tell the side effects are pretty minimal in relation to most other diets. Not only that but these side effects are easily reversed with a little bit of attention on your part.

*For the first few weeks of your diet your body will be adjusting and purging itself of all the built up toxins in your body. During this time frame, you may feel ill or unwell at times. This is completely normal.

Once your body has rid itself of all the excess toxins and sugars in your body you'll notice an increase in energy and noticeable improvement in your overall well-being.

Five Rules for Rapid Weight Loss

For the success of the Mediterranean Diet, you need to adhere to the following rules:

Rule #1: Ensure That You Focus On Plant-Based Foods

When preparing your meals, ensure that you that the seasonal fresh ingredients that include vegetables, fruits, whole grains, legumes, and nuts.

Rule #2: Adapt to Using Healthy Oil

When on a Mediterranean Diet, fats are very important. But ensure you are ingesting the correct ones by using natural oils instead of butter.

Rule #3: Get Good Protein Selections

Do not consume red meat or beef on a daily basis. Instead you can enjoy once a week. Get use to alternative sources like poultry, fish, eggs, or cheese.

Rule #4: Go Local and Ensure Your Ingredients are Fresh

In the Mediterranean, nations experience different seasons. Most foods are grown locally and will always be fresh from the market or store. It ensures that your meals are prepared with the available ingredients depending on the season making them fresh and healthy.

Rule #5: Eat Smaller Amounts

To enjoy the rich, delicious, and healthy Mediterranean foods, control your intake. Eat small bites to ensure that you taste more food, ingest less and enjoy all the health benefits.

Top Hints for Your Success

If you are interested in applying the Mediterranean diet to your life to lose weight then these general dieting tips paired with the Mediterranean diet eating habits will help you maximize your weight loss.

Eat Slowly

It takes twenty minutes for your food to start digesting and give you a feeling of fullness after you eat a meal. Therefore, slow down and chew your food so that you can actually taste it and enjoy the flavor. If you tend to eat fast, you may find that you eat more because it takes that twenty minutes to get your internal system fired up.

Drink Water Before Your Meal

Try drinking a full eight-ounce glass of water before you sit down to eat a meal. Sometimes thirst can be mistaken for a feeling of hunger. Drinking a glass of water before you eat can get the digestion process started quicker which can cause you to eat less during a meal.

Split Your Plate Into Three Sections

Visually split your plate in half then split one of those halves in two. This makes three sections.... two small ones and one big one.

The big section is for vegetables and the two smaller sections are for your starches and proteins.

You can use this as a measuring guide when you go out to eat or want to transition your dinner plate into healthier portions.

You will receive the highest levels of phytonutrients from vegetables so that is why vegetables occupy the largest section of the plate.

Exercise

Adhere to the lowest, most foundational level of the Mediterranean pyramid which is a daily activity. Do your best to get thirty minutes of exercise every day.

Change the Way You Think About Food

See vegetables and fruits as snacks. Slice your vegetables into ready to eat snack sizes and wash your fruits when you bring them home from the store so that they are ready to grab as a quick snack when you're feeling hungry.

Always have a jar of mixed nuts within your reach in the kitchen counter and eat a handful of those along with your vegetable or fruit snack.

Replace butter and margarine with olive oil. I especially like to use olive oil when grilling sandwiches or toasting my breads where at one time I only used butter or margarine.

Prepackage Snacks

Prepackage snacks into portion sizes rather than eating from the full container. This can prevent overeating. When you pre-allocate how much of a snack you're going to eat then you're helping yourself stay disciplined.

Snack Two or Three Times a Day

Enjoy two or three snacking times a day where you eat a serving of fruit or vegetables with no salt or sugar added. Schedule a snack in the morning, afternoon, and before bed.

Replace Cakes and Cookies

Replace frequent cake and cookie binges with a serving of popcorn cooked in olive oil and sprinkled with parmesan cheese or garlic powder rather than salt and butter.

Buy Smaller Plates and Bowls

When you fill up a smaller plate or bowl you can still get the satisfaction of having a full plate or bowl. With a smaller bowl/plate, you can feel satisfied but still be able to eat in healthy portions that adhere to the Mediterranean diet food pyramid.

Replace Saturated Fats with Monounsaturated Fats

Give your weight loss program the super-charged fuel it needs by replacing your saturated fats with monounsaturated fats. The Mediterranean diet replaces a standard bad fat diet with high levels of healthy monounsaturated fats that raise good cholesterol levels.

Learn a Well-Balanced Eating Plan

The longer you adhere to the Mediterranean diet the more energy and vitality you will receive.

The Mediterranean diet offers a well-balanced eating plan that includes the correct amount of each food group.

14-Day Meal Plan

Day 1

Breakfast: Oatmeal with Yogurt & Egg

Lunch: Tuscan Style Tuna Salad

Dinner: Mediterranean Grilled Chicken Kebabs

Dessert/Snack: Banana-Strawberry Smoothie

Day 2

Breakfast: Baked Eggs with Spinach

Lunch: Mediterranean Egg Salad

Dinner: Seafood Linguine

Dessert/Snack: Honey Pistachio Roasted Pears

Day 3

Breakfast: Quinoa & Dried Fruit

Lunch: Mexican Tuna Salad

Dinner: Mediterranean Stuffed Chicken Breasts

Dessert/Snack: Evoo Cake

Day 4

Breakfast: Eggs & Hash & Cheese

Lunch: Creamy Paninis

Dinner: Grilled Steak and Sweet Potatoes

Dessert/Snack: Medjool Date Truffles

Day 5

Breakfast: Veggie Breakfast Bowl

Lunch: Spinach with Garbanzo Beans

Dinner: Spinach and Feta Pita Bake

Dessert/Snack: Greek Yogurt

Day 6

Breakfast: Apple Peanut Butter Oatmeal

Lunch: Pressed Picnic Sandwich
Dinner: Gnocchi, Tomatoes, and Pancetta
Dessert/Snack: Figs with Blue Cheese
Day 7
Breakfast: Edamame & Sweet Pea Hummus
Lunch: Roasted Peppers with Broiled Feta & Olives
Dinner: Chicken Costa Brava
Dessert/Snack: Parmesan Herbed Walnuts
Week 2
Day 1
Breakfast: Muffin Pan Frittatas
Lunch: Broccolini Almond Pizza
Dinner: Mediterranean Chicken Couscous
Dessert/Snack: Chia Seed Pumpkin Pudding
Day 2
Breakfast: Avocado & Egg Breakfast Sandwich
Lunch: Greek Orzo Salad
Dinner: Mediterranean Flounder
Dessert/Snack: Summer Fruit Granita
Day 3
Breakfast: Mediterranean Frittata
Lunch: Mediterranean Quinoa Salad
Dinner: Naked Lasagna
Dessert/Snack: Sweet Ricotta & Strawberry Parfaits
Day 4
Breakfast: Mediterranean Breakfast Sandwich
Lunch: Spinach & Tuna Salad
Dinner: Lemon-Garlic Shrimp
Dessert/Snack: Avocado & Blueberry Bang

Day 5
Breakfast: Mediterranean Breakfast Wrap
Lunch: Chicken Souvlaki with Tzatziki
Dinner: Penne and Chicken
Dessert/Snack: Peanut Butter Popcorn
Day 6
Breakfast: Mediterranean Egg Scramble
Lunch: Mediterranean Pasta Salad
Dinner: Seared Salmon and White Beans
Dessert/Snack: Dried Figs with Ricotta & Walnuts
Day 7
Breakfast: Breakfast Couscous
Lunch: Greek Bruschetta
Dinner: Salmon Panzanella
Dessert/Snack: Chocolate Mousse with Olive Oil

Breakfast Recipes

Oatmeal with Yogurt & Egg

Servings: 1

Ingredients:

- ⅓ c. oats
- ⅓ c. low-fat milk
- 1 egg
- ¼ tsp. cinnamon
- ¼ c. yogurt
- ¼ c. slashed apple
- Salt
- Sugar

Directions:

1. Blend the milk and egg. Mix in all ingredients except yogurt and apple.
2. Microwave until the liquid is evaporated, (for about 2 minutes).
3. Spread yogurt and apples on top of oatmeal.

Nutritional Information: 320 calories, 46g Carbs, 9g fat, 17g protein

Baked Eggs with Spinach

Servings: 4

Ingredients:

- 4 eggs
- 1 package frozen spinach
- ¼ c. shredded Cheddar cheese
- ¼ c. chunky salsa

Directions:

1. Preheat oven to 325°F.
2. Put equal amount of spinach into 4 custard cup. Make a well in the middle by pressing down with your fingers.
3. Add an egg into each indentation. Spoon salsa and shredded cheese on the top.
4. Cook for 20 min.

Nutritional Information: 120 calories, 4g carbs, 7g fat, 10g protein

Quinoa & Dried Fruit

Servings: 4

Ingredients:

- 3 c. water
- 1 c. quinoa
- ¼ c. walnuts
- 8 dried apricots
- 4 dried figs
- 1 tsp. cinnamon

Directions:

1. In a pot, mix water and quinoa and let simmer for 15 minutes, until the water evaporates.
2. Chop dried fruit.
3. When quinoa is cooked, stir in all other ingredients.
4. Serve cold. Add milk, if desired.

Nutritional Information: 44g carbs, 7g fat, 13g protein, 285 calories

Eggs & Hash & Cheese

Servings: 1

Ingredients:

- 1 egg
- ½ c. shredded hash browns
- 2 tbsps. cheddar cheese
- Salt
- Pepper

Directions:

1. Grease a microwaveable bowl with olive oil spray and fill with hashbrowns. Microwave for 1 minute, and add salt and pepper to taste.
2. Stir in an egg and beat well. Microwave for 45 seconds.
3. Sprinkle cheese over the top.

Nutritional Information: 7g carbs, 14g fat, 15g protein, 210 calories

Veggie Breakfast Bowl

Servings: 1

Ingredients:

- 1 egg
- 1 tbsp. water
- 2 tbsps. shredded mozzarella cheese
- 2 tbsps. diced mushrooms
- ¼ c. baby spinach
- 2 tbsps. cherry tomatoes

Directions:

1. Mix all ingredients excluding the cheese in a greased microwaveable bowl.
2. Microwave for 1 minute or until the egg is cooked.
3. Sprinkle shredded cheese over the top.

Nutritional Information: 2g carbs, 6g fat, 10g protein, 100 calories

Apple Peanut Butter Oatmeal

Servings: 4

Ingredients:

- 1 c. steel cut oats
- ¼ c. brown sugar
- ½ tsp. cinnamon
- ¼ c. peanut butter
- 1 tsp. vanilla extract
- 2 diced apples
- Salt

Directions:

1. Grease a slow cooker with cooking spray.
2. Add all ingredients to the crockpot except apples, mix well.
3. Add apples to the top of the mixture and cook on low for 8 hours.

Nutritional Information: 50g carbs, 11g fat, 10g protein, 320 calories

Edamame & Sweet Pea Hummus

Servings: 2

Ingredients:

- ½ c. edamame
- ½ c. peas
- 2 tbsps. Tahini
- 1 minced garlic clove
- 2 tbsps. chopped mint
- 3 tbsps. olive oil
- 2 wheat tortillas
- 2 eggs

Directions:

1. Blend first 5 ingredients and 1 Tbsp. of olive oil in a food processor. Spread evenly over the wheat tortillas.
2. Coat pan with remaining olive oil and cook the eggs. When ready, put one egg on each tortilla.

Nutritional Information: 35g carbs, 30g fat, 20g protein, 460 calories

Muffin Pan Frittatas

Servings: 6

Ingredients:

- 6 eggs
- ½ c. milk
- 1 c. cheddar cheese
- ¾ c. chopped zucchini
- ¼ c. chopped red bell pepper
- 2 tbsps. sliced red onion
- Pepper

Directions:

1. Preheat oven to 350°F.
2. Mix the milk, eggs, and pepper. Then mix in other ingredients.
3. Spray cooking spray on a muffin tin and distribute the prepared mixture evenly between the cups. Bake for 15 min.

Nutritional Information: 3g carbs, 10g fat, 12g protein, 165 calories

Avocado & Egg Breakfast Sandwich

Servings: 2

Ingredients:

- 4 toasted bread slices
- 1 avocado
- 12 steamed asparagus spears
- 1 sliced hard-boiled egg
- Olive oil
- Pepper
- Sea salt
- Dijon mustard

Directions:

1. Peel and mash the avocado and toast the bread.
2. Prepare the sandwich by using the mustard with a layer of the avocado.
3. Add the asparagus spears and eggs. Give it a drizzle of oil along with some salt and pepper. Close and enjoy.

Nutritional Information: 283.6 calories, 11.5g fat, 31g carbs, 10.9g protein

Mediterranean Frittata

Servings: 6

Ingredients:

- ½ c. diced tomatoes
- ½ c. milk
- 6 eggs
- ¼ c. of each
- ¼ c. Spanish
- ¼ c. Kalamata
- 1 c. chopped spinach
- ½ tsp. pepper
- 1 tsp. oregano
- 1 tsp. salt
- ¼ c. crumbled feta

Directions:

1. Program the oven temperature to 400°F.
2. Grease the chosen dish, and whisk the milk and eggs.
3. Combine all of the fixings, mixing well.
4. Bake for 15-20 minutes. The eggs will be set and ready to serve.

Nutritional Information: 242 Calories, 7g Carbs, 19g Fat, 12g Protein

Mediterranean Breakfast Sandwich

Servings: 1

Ingredients:

- 1 Heirloom Tomato
- 1 Onion
- 2 slices of Bread
- ¼ Zucchini
- 1 Egg
- 1 tbsp. Basil
- Salt

Directions:

1. Begin by thinly slicing the onion, zucchini, tomato, and basil leaves.
2. Place the olive oil into the pan on medium heat and add egg. The style of egg is up to you.
3. Meanwhile, toast your bread slices in a toaster.
4. Place one slice of bread of bread onto a plate and lay the egg on top.
5. In the pan, set the zucchini and onion and allow them to brown. This should take only a few minutes.
6. On the other slice of bread, layer your tomato and basil.
7. Once your onion and zucchini are soft, layer them on top of the tomato and basil.
8. Finally, layer the bread pieces on top of one another and your sandwich is complete!

Nutritional Information: 242 calories, 25g carbs, 12g fat, 13g protein

Mediterranean Breakfast Wrap

Servings: 2

Ingredients:

- ¼ c. red pepper
- ¼ c. onion
- 1 tomato
- ½ c. baby spinach
- 1 c. egg substitute
- 1½ tsps. fresh basil
- 2 wheat tortillas
- 2 tbsps. feta cheese
- 1 tbsp. olive oil

Directions:

1. Begin by heating the olive oil into your pan and then add your pepper and onion.
2. Continue cooking the onion and pepper over medium heat until soft.
3. Next, add the egg substitute with the spices and cook until eggs are as desired.
4. Once the egg is cooked, you will want to place the spinach, tomato, and egg into the wrap.
5. Add the crumbled feta cheese onto the wrap and your meal is complete!

Nutritional Information: 448 calories, 27g fat, 41g carbs, 15g protein

Mediterranean Egg Scramble

Servings: 4

Ingredients:

- 4 Slices bread
- 6 Eggs
- ¼ diced red bell pepper
- 3 sliced potatoes
- 8 chopped black olives
- ¼ c. fresh ricotta cheese
- ¼ c. parsley
- 5 tsps. butter
- 1 tsp. olive oil

Directions:

1. Begin by heating the olive oil and butter in a pan over medium-high heat.
2. Once the olive oil and butter are simmering, add the sliced potatoes into the pan and sauté for 15 minutes.
3. Once potatoes are golden, add the bell pepper and olives. Allow these to cook for about 4 minutes.
4. When this mixture is complete, take a medium bowl and whisk your eggs, ricotta, and parsley together.
5. In your pan, you will want to pour the egg mixture over the potato mixture.
6. Stir the mixture every 30 seconds so that the mixture is firm but not dry. Do this for about 3 minutes.
7. Once the mixture is complete, place it over your toasted bread and your meal is complete!

Nutritional Information: 324 Calories, 24g fat, 20g protein, 7g carbs

Breakfast Couscous

Servings: 4

Ingredients:

- 1 c. uncooked whole-wheat couscous
- 3 c. low-fat milk
- ½ c. currants, dried
- 1 (2 in.) cinnamon stick
- ½ c. apricots, dried
- ¼ tsp. salt
- 6 tsps. dark brown sugar, divided
- 4 tsps. melted butter divided

Directions:

1. Using a medium-high burner on the stovetop, place a large saucepan and add the cinnamon stick and milk. Heat it until you see bubble formations along the edges. (Do not bring to a boil.)
2. Remove the pan from the burner and blend in the apricots, couscous, salt, currants, and four teaspoons of the brown sugar.
3. Close the lid and let it rest for 15 minutes. Take the top off and throw away the cinnamon stick.
4. Serve evenly in four bowls and garnish with the rest of the brown sugar and a teaspoon of melted butter.

Nutritional Information: 306 calories, 6g fat, 55g carbs, 11g protein

Lunch Recipes

Broccolini Almond Pizza

Servings: 6

Ingredients

- 1 lb. homemade pizza dough
- 2/3 c. marinara sauce/32 oz. drained & crushed whole tomatoes
- ½ c. crumbled feta
- 8 oz. broccolini
- 2 c. shredded mozzarella cheese
- 1 tsp. EVOO
- ¼ c. sliced almonds
- Basil leaves
- Red pepper flakes

Directions:

1. Set the oven temperature to 500°F. using the upper third of the oven.
2. Prepare the dough by spreading the sauce over the two pizzas. Add the feta and mozzarella.
3. Prepare the broccolini in a large pot with a few inches of hot water. Trim the ends and add them to the boiling water. Allow to boil and let it steam one minute. Drain and pay them dry.
4. Toss the broccolini into the oil until coated evenly. Add over the pizzas and sprinkle with the almonds. Bake 12 minutes or until done.
5. Slice, garnish as you like, and serve.

Nutritional Information: 297 calories, 12.2g fat, 36g carbs, 14.3g protein

Greek Bruschetta

Servings: 6

Bread Ingredients

- 1 tbsp. olive oil
- 1 large garlic clove
- 1 whole-grain baguette

Tomato Topping Ingredients

- ¼ c. Chopped fresh basil
- ¼ c. chopped Kalamata olives, pitted
- 2 c. cherry tomatoes, quartered
- 1 tbsp. Balsamic vinegar
- 1 tsp. Olive oil
- 1 tsp. dried oregano
- Pinch of pepper
- Pinch of Salt

Directions:

1. Set the oven in advance to 425°F.
2. Slice the baguette into ½-inch slices. Rub with garlic. Brush with the oil and add in a single layer in a large (with rim) baking tin.
3. Bake five to eight minutes on each side.
4. Meanwhile, mix the ingredients for the bruschetta. Toss to evenly coat and adjust seasonings to your taste.
5. Serve with the tomatoes to the side in a dish. It will keep in the fridge for two days.
6. Enjoy for a quick lunch or snack!

Nutritional Information: 127 calories, 7g fat, 13g carbs, 3g protein

Greek Orzo Salad

Servings: 8

Ingredients

- 1 c. orzo pasta, uncooked
- ½ c. freshly minced parsley
- 6 tsps. divided olive oil
- 1 onion, finely chopped
- 1½ tsps. Oregano, dried
- 1/3 c. red wine vinegar
- Salt

Directions:

1. Cook and drain the orzo. Add it to a serving dish with two teaspoons of the oil.
2. In another dish mix the parsley, onion, salt, vinegar, sugar, rest of the oil, oregano, and pepper. Pour over the orzo and place in the fridge two to 24 hours.
3. Right before the time for lunch, blend in the olives, tomatoes, cucumber, and cheese. Serve with a smile!

Nutritional Information: 399 calories, 12.7g fat, 55g carbs, 16.2g protein

Mediterranean Egg Salad

Servings: 4

Ingredients:

- 8 eggs, hard-boiled
- ½ c. Chopped cucumber
- ½ c. Red onion
- ½ c. tomatoes, Sun-dried
- ¼ c. olives
- Splash – lemon juice
- ½ c. plain Greek yogurt
- ¼ tsp. cumin
- 1½ tsps. oregano
- Freshly cracked black pepper
- ½ tsp. sea salt

Directions:

1. Drain off the excess of oil from the tomatoes. Chop the veggies and eggs.
2. Combine the eggs with the tomatoes, onion, olives, and cucumber. Stir in the spices, lemon juice, and yogurt.
3. Refrigerate for about one week.

Nutritional Information: 240 calories, 23g fat, 3g carbs, 7g protein

Mediterranean Pasta Salad

Servings: 4

Ingredients

- 8 oz. multigrain farfalle
- 2 tsps. olive oil
- 1 lemon – Zest & juice
- 13.5 oz. artichoke hearts
- 8 oz. mozzarella cheese, freshly chopped
- ¼ c. chopped Red bell pepper, roasted
- ¼ c. freshly chopped parsley
- ½ c. frozen peas

Directions:

1. Prepare the pasta according to package directions (omit fat and salt).
2. Combine the zest, juiced lemon, and oil in a mixing container.
3. Drain and chop the artichoke. Add it and the rest of the fixings (cheese, parsley, and peppers). Toss well.
4. Add the peas to a colander. Pour the pasta and water over it when it's done. Shake to drain (don't run water over). Add to the mixture and toss.
5. Serve and enjoy at room temperature or warmed.

Nutritional Information: 159 calories, 3.5g fat, 26g carbs, 5.7g protein

Mediterranean Quinoa Salad

Servings: 4

Ingredients

- 1 c. uncooked quinoa
- 1/3 c. red wine vinegar
- 2 c. water
- ¼ c. olive oil
- 1 red pepper, diced
- 1 red onion, diced
- ½ c. Kalamata olives
- 1 juiced lemon
- ½ c. freshly chopped cilantro
- ½ tsp. black pepper
- 1 tsp. salt
- ½ c. crumbled feta cheese
- 2 Roma tomatoes

Directions:

1. First, you will need to dice the tomatoes, onions, and peppers.
2. Prepare a pot of water (med. heat) to boil, and add the quinoa. Reduce the heat and cook for 15-20 minutes. The water should be completely absorbed. Fluff and cool for five minutes.
3. Add the vinegar and oil—as the quinoa comes to room temperature.
4. Blend in the tomatoes, onion, olives, red peppers, cilantro, pepper, and salt. Gently blend and add the feta cheese. Refrigerate for about two hours so the flavors can intertwine.
5. Before serving, give it a drizzle of lemon juice.

Mexican Tuna Salad

Servings: 2

Ingredients

- 6 oz. chunk light tuna in water
- 2 scallions, minced
- 1 green pepper, minced
- ¼ c. prepared green salsa
- 6 chopped pimento olives, stuffed
- 1 tbsp. lime juice
- 2 tbsps. mayonnaise, reduced-fat
- ½ tsp. ground cumin
- Ground black pepper

Directions:

1. Combine all of the fixings in a dish. Season with the pepper and salt.
2. Enjoy however you like!

Nutritional Information: 188 calories, 9.6g fat, 19.7g carbs, 10.5g protein

Spinach & Tuna Salad

Servings: 1

Ingredients

- 1½ tbsps. Water
- 1½ tbsps. Lemon juice
- 1½ tbsps. Tahini
- 5 oz. chunk light tuna
- 4 Kalamata olives, pitted
- 2 tbsps. Parsley
- 2 tbsps. Feta cheese
- 2 c. baby spinach
- 1 orange

Directions:

1. Drain the tuna and chop the olives. Whisk the water, juice, and tahini together. Blend in the rest of the fixings – stirring well to combine.
2. Serve over the baby spinach with the orange peeled and sliced on the side.

Nutritional Information: 203 calories, 9g fat, 14.7g carbs, 9.5g protein

Tuscan Style Tuna Salad

Servings: 4

Ingredients

- 15 oz. small white beans
- 6 oz. drained chunk light tuna
- 10 cherry tomatoes, quartered
- 4 trimmed scallions, sliced
- ¼ tsp. salt
- 2 tbsps. lemon juice
- Pepper

Directions:

1. Combine all of the fixings in a covered container.
2. Stir gently and refrigerate until ready to eat.

Nutritional Information: 322 calories, 8.2g fat, 32.9g carbs, 30g protein

Chicken Souvlaki with Tzatziki

Servings: 6

Ingredients:

- 2 tbsps. lemon juice
- 14 oz. Greek yogurt
- 2 tsps. chopped oregano leaves
- ¼ c. white dry wine
- ¼ c. olive oil
- ½ tsp. pepper - divided
- 1 tsp. kosher salt
- 2 lb. skinned breasts
- 4 minced garlic cloves
- 2 tsps. distilled white vinegar
- ½ c. cucumber

Directions:

1. Cut the chicken into ½-inch cubes, and coarsely shred the cucumber.
2. Set the grill between 450°F and 550°F.
3. Blend the wine, oil, chicken, oregano, lemon juice, cloves, ¼ teaspoon of the pepper, and the salt in a mixing bowl.
4. Use eight metal skewers to prepare the chicken for cooking. Grill for approximately 10-12 minutes.
5. Remove any excess moisture from the cucumbers with paper towels, and put them into a medium dish. Mix in the yogurt, garlic, vinegar, and pepper with the cucumbers.
6. Serve with warm pita bread and the chicken.

Nutritional Information: 294 calories, 5.2g fat, 42.1g carbs, 22.2g protein

Creamy Paninis

Servings: 4

Ingredients:

- 8 slices whole grain bread
- ½ c. mayonnaise
- ¼ c. fresh basil leaves
- 7-oz. roasted red peppers
- 2 tbsps. chopped black olives
- 1 sliced zucchini
- 4 slices provolone cheese

Directions:

1. Finely chop the basil leaves.
2. In a small dish, mix the finely chopped olives with the mayonnaise.
3. Spread it on the slices of bread with the peppers, zucchini, and provolone. Top with the remainder of the slices.
4. Place mayonnaise on the outside of each sandwich.
5. On the stovetop using medium heat, place the sandwiches on a grill pan or skillet. Brown each of the sandwiches for approximately four minutes.
6. What a treat with all of that melted cheese!

Nutritional Information: 300 calories, 44g fat, 33g carbs, 26g protein

Pressed Picnic Sandwich

Servings: 6

Ingredients:

- 1 small zucchini
- 1 small eggplant
- 1 small yellow squash
- 3 tbsp. olive oil
- 1 large ciabatta bread
- 1/3 c. tapenade
- 1/3 c. pesto
- 2 jars sliced and roasted red peppers
- 18 oz. mozzarella
- 2 tbsp. balsamic vinegar

Directions:

1. Slice the veggies lengthwise into ¼- inch slices. Drain and slice the mozzarella. Warm up the grill or grill pan (med.-high).
2. Use a brush to lightly oil the veggies. Grill 3-4 minutes for each side, until softened and charred. Arrange on a platter.
3. Prepare the bread with pesto on one side and the tapenade on the other.
4. Layer the veggies and mozzarella on one side and drizzle with the rest of the oil and vinegar. Shake the pepper and salt as desired.
5. Press the sandwich together and wrap tightly using plastic wrap. Refrigerate on a baking tin overnight or at least two hours. Apply a heavy skillet to 'squash' the sandwich.
6. When ready to serve, unwrap and slice.

Nutritional Information: 766 calories, 31g fat, 60g carbs, 42g protein

Roasted Peppers with Broiled Feta & Olives

Servings: 6

Ingredients:

- 1 yellow
- 1 red pepper
- 1 Vidalia onion
- 1 tsp. olive oil
- 1 head garlic
- 1 tbsp. regular capers or 8 caper berries
- 12 green olives

- 8 anchovies
- 12 Kalamata olives
- Juice of 1 lemon
- 8 oz. feta cheese
- ¼ c. chives
- ¼ c. mint
- ¼ c. dill
- ¼ c. parsley

Directions:

1. Slice the peppers into halves, lengthwise. Separate the cloves and peel. Slice the onion into rounds. Warm up the oven to 400°F.
2. Arrange the garlic, onion, and peppers on a baking sheet. Brush them with some oil and bake (approximately 20 min.). Take from the oven, place on a covered dish or under some tight-fitting wrap.
3. Reset the broiler setting in the oven. Use a baking sheet or casserole dish to crumble the feta. Broil until it bubbles - approximately two minutes.
4. Blend the remaining ingredients in a large mixing dish. Combine the onions, garlic, and peppers - tossing well.
5. Take the cheese from the broiler and spoon into the serving plates. Garnish with the pepper mixture.

Nutritional Information: 221 calories, 20g fat, 4g carbs, 8g protein

Spinach with Garbanzo Beans

Servings: 4

Ingredients:

- 1 tbsp. olive oil
- 4 minced garlic cloves
- ½ diced onion
- 10 oz. chopped spinach
- 12 oz. garbanzo beans
- ½ tsp. cumin
- ½ tsp. salt

Directions:

1. In a skillet, warm the olive oil over medium-low heat.
2. Then add the onions, and garlic and cook until the onions are translucent. About 5 minutes.
3. Stir in spinach, cumin, salt and garbanzo beans. Use your spoon to slightly mash the beans as the mixture cooks.
4. Allow to cook until thoroughly heated.

Nutritional Information: 90 calories, 4g fat, 11g carbs, 4g protein

Dinner

Mediterranean Stuffed Chicken Breasts

Servings: 8

Ingredients:

- 8 oz. chicken breasts
- 1 Large red bell pepper
- 2 tbsps. chopped Kalamata olives
- ¼ c. crumbled feta cheese
- 1 tbsp. fresh basil

Directions:

1. Begin by preheating your broiler.
2. On a chopping block, start cutting your bell pepper in half, lengthwise and get rid of all of the membrane and seeds.
3. On a baking sheet, place the pepper halves skin side up and flatten them with your hand.
4. Place the peppers into the oven and broil for about 15 minutes or until they have blackened.
5. Once they are prepared, place the peppers into a ziplock bag and allow them to sit for about 15 minutes.
6. When the time has passed, peel the peppers and chop them.
7. When this is done, place a pan on your grill over medium-high heat and place your cheese, olives, basil, and bell pepper.
8. With your chicken, you will want to slice a horizontal slit through the thickest part of the chicken to form some sort of a pocket.
9. Once this is done, place the pepper mixture into each of your chicken breasts and then close the pocket with a wooden toothpick.
10. Sprinkle pepper and salt over the chicken and place the chicken on a grill rack.
11. Grill each side for about 6 minutes on both sides or until it is thoroughly cooked.

12. Once cooked, allow the chicken to stand for about 10 minutes. Your meal is ready to be served once it is cooled!

Nutritional Information: 210 calories, 5.9g fat, 35.2g protein, 1.8g carbs

Mediterranean Grilled Chicken Kebabs

Servings: 8

Ingredients:

- 2 lbs. chicken thighs
- 1 c. pomegranate-orange dressing
- 2 large oranges
- ¼ c. chopped mint
- ¼ tsp. salt
- ¼ tsp. black pepper
- Cooking spray

Directions:

1. Begin by combining a ½ cup of the dressing with the chicken in a large zip-top plastic bag. You will want to marinate this mixture for about 30 minutes in the fridge.
2. Once the time has passed, prepare your grill to medium-high heat.
3. On a separate cutting board, cut the orange into 8 wedges and cut those wedges crosswise into three pieces.
4. Take your chicken out from the bag and thread the orange pieces and chicken pieces onto the skewers.
5. If desired, sprinkle with and pepper for extra seasoning.
6. Arrange the kebabs on the rack and grill each side for about 5 minutes or until the chicken is cooked thoroughly.
7. Place the finished kebabs on a plate and sprinkle with mint for a nice final touch!

Nutritional Information: 208 calories, 11.3g fat, 21.2g protein, 5.2g carbs

Mediterranean Chicken Couscous

Servings: 8

Ingredients:

- 3 c. chopped chicken
- 1 ¼ c. chicken broth
- 1 Pint grape tomatoes
- 1 tsp. lemon rind
- 1 ½ tbsps. fresh lemon juice
- 1 5.6 oz. package of toasted pine nut couscous mix
- ¼ c. chopped fresh basil
- 1 4oz. package feta cheese
- ¼ tsp. pepper

Directions:

1. You will want to begin this by heating the chicken broth and the seasoning packet from the couscous in a microwave for three to five minutes while on high.
2. Once the broth is boiling, mix it with the couscous in a large bowl and allow it to stand for about five minutes.
3. Once the time has passed, fluff the couscous with a fork and stir in the chicken.
4. When this is complete, mix in your spices and your meal is complete!

Nutritional Information: 334 calories, 10.9g fat, 35.8g carbs, 20.9g protein

Lemon-Garlic Shrimp

Servings: 12

Ingredients:

- 1¼ lbs. shrimp
- 3 tbsps. minced garlic
- ¼ c. lemon juice
- ¼ c. fresh parsley
- 2 tbsps. olive oil
- ½ tsp. salt
- ½ tsp. pepper

Directions:

1. Begin by placing a small skillet over medium heat. Put your garlic and oil in for about a minute.
2. Next, add the parsley, lemon juice, and the salt and pepper.
3. Last, place the shrimp into a large bowl and place the mixture over the shrimp.
4. Chill until ready to serve!

Nutritional Information: 130 calories, 3.52g fat, 2g carbs, 22.65g protein

Seafood Linguine

Servings: 4

Ingredients:

- 8 oz. tilapia
- 8 oz. dry sea scallops
- 12 Littleneck Clams
- 8 oz. whole-wheat linguine
- 2 tbsps. olive oil
- 28 oz. diced tomatoes
- 1 tbsp. chopped shallot
- 4 chopped garlic cloves
- 1 tbsp. chopped marjoram
- ¼ c. Parmesan cheese
- ½ c. white wine
- ½ tsp. salt
- ¼ tsp. pepper

Directions:

1. Place water in a large pot a boil. Once boiling, add pasta and cook for 8 to 10 minutes or until tender. Be sure to drain and rinse after.
2. Meanwhile, heat oil in a large skillet over medium heat. Once the oil is simmering, add the garlic and shallot and stir for about a minute.
3. When garlic is soft, increase the heat to medium-high and add in the white wine, tomatoes, and the salt and pepper. Allow this mixture to cook for about a minute.
4. Once this time has passed, you will want to add in your clams and cook them for about 2 minutes.
5. Last, stir in your scallops, fish, and marjoram and cook these for 3 to 5 minutes.
6. Soon, you can spoon in the sauce over your pasta and sprinkle with Parmesan cheese for the perfect final touch. Enjoy your meal!

Nutritional Information: 830 calories, 28g fat, 92g carbs, 45g protein

Seared Salmon and White Beans

Servings: 2

Ingredients:

- 8 oz. salmon fillet
- 1 Medium tomato
- 1 Small bulb of fennel
- 15 oz. white beans
- 3 tsps. olive oil
- ¼ c. dry white wine
- 1½ tsps. Dijon mustard
- 1 tsp. fennel seed
- ¼ tsp. pepper

Directions:

1. Begin by heating a tablespoon of the olive oil in a large skillet over medium heat.
2. Add in the sliced fennel and cook for about 6 minutes or until lightly browned.
3. When this is done, stir in the white wine, tomato, and beans for about 3 minutes.
4. After the mixture is done cooking, transfer it into a bowl and stir in the chopped fennel, mustard, and a 1/8 teaspoon of pepper.
5. Before continuing, rinse and dry the pan you just used.
6. In a small bowl, combine the fennel seed and a 1/8 teaspoon of pepper and then sprinkle the mixture on both sides of the salmon.
7. In the pan, heat up the remaining two teaspoons of olive oil over medium-high heat and then add the salmon. Cook for 3-6 minutes or until golden brown. Be sure to cook both sides of the salmon.
8. Last, place the beans onto a plate and top with the salmon. Your meal is complete!

Nutritional Information: 485 calories, 23g fat, 39g carbs, 35g protein

Grilled Steak and Sweet Potatoes

Servings: 2

Ingredients:

- 8 oz. strip steak
- 1 Sweet potato
- 1 sliced onion
- ½ tsp. allspice
- ¼ tsp. cinnamon
- ¼ tsp. coriander
- ½ tsp. cumin
- ¼ tsp. cayenne pepper
- ½ tsp. ground ginger
- ½ tsp. salt
- 2 tsps. canola oil
- ½ tsp. grated orange zest

Directions:

1. Begin by preheating your grill to high.
2. In a medium bowl, combine the allspice, cinnamon, cayenne pepper, coriander, cumin, ginger and salt. Next, you will want to sprinkle your steak with 2 ¼ teaspoons of the mixture.
3. Next, add the sweet potato and onion into the bowl and coat completely with the spice mixture.
4. On a baking plate, add some foil on top and coat with cooking spray. You will want to layer the sweet potato mixture onto the tin foil and then fold the foil until you can pinch it together and seal the packet.
5. You will want to place the packet on the hottest part of your grill and cook both sides for about 5 minutes.
6. On the same grill, cook your steaks for about 3 to 4 minutes on each side.
7. For the final meal, serve the steak over the sweet potatoes and your meal is complete.

Nutritional Information: 376 calories, 19g fat, 34g protein, 16g carbs

Naked Lasagna

Servings: 4

Ingredients:

- 8 oz. whole-wheat rotini
- 3 sliced garlic cloves
- 8 c. baby spinach
- 8 oz. sliced white mushrooms
- 1 chopped onion
- 14 oz. diced tomatoes
- ¾ c. ricotta cheese
- ½ tsp. crushed red pepper
- ½ tsp. Salt
- ¼ tsp. Pepper

Directions:

1. Place water in a large pot and boil and add in the pasta. You will want to cook for 8 to 10 minutes or until the pasta is tender.
2. In a large skillet, place your onions and garlic over medium heat and cook until they begin to brown. This should take around 3 minutes.
3. Once the time has passed, add in the mushrooms along with the salt and pepper and stir for 4 to 6 minutes.
4. When this is done, add in the spinach, tomatoes, and crushed red pepper. Increase your heat to medium-high and cook for about 4 minutes.
5. Last, you will want to add in the sauce with the pasta and add the ricotta cheese for a final touch.

Nutritional Information: 370 calories, 13g fat, 47g carbs, 18g protein

Gnocchi, Tomatoes, and Pancetta

Servings: 4

Ingredients:

- 1 lb. gnocchi
- 4 oz. watercress
- 2 oz. pancetta
- 2 chopped tomatoes
- 3 minced garlic cloves
- 2 tsps. red-wine vinegar
- ¼ tsp. crushed red pepper
- ½ tsp. sugar
- ¼ tsp. salt
- 1/3 c. grated Parmesan cheese

Directions:

1. Place water in a large pot and bring to a boil.
2. In a large skillet over medium heat, you will want to cook the pancetta for about 5 minutes.
3. Once it has changed color, add in the garlic and cook the mixture for another 30 seconds.
4. When the garlic is simmering, add in the crushed red pepper, sugar, and tomatoes for 5 minutes.
5. Last, stir in the vinegar and salt and then remove the mixture from the heat.
6. In the boiling pot of water, place the gnocchi and cook for 3 to 5 minutes or until it is floating.
7. Drain the gnocchi over the watercress and then add the gnocchi to the sauce in the pan.
8. Be sure to toss it well to make sure all of the ingredients are combined.
9. Last, dish the meal into separate plates and decorate with Parmesan cheese if desired.

Nutritional Information: 377 calories, 64g carbs, 7g fat, 14g protein

Penne and Chicken

Servings: 4

Ingredients:

- 16 oz. penne noodles
- 1 ½ tbsps. butter
- ½ c. red onion, chopped
- 2 minced garlic cloves
- 1 lb. boneless and skinless chicken breast.
- 14 oz. chopped artichoke hearts, drained
- 1 chopped tomato
- ½ c. feta cheese, crumbled
- 3 tbsps. chopped parsley
- 2 tbsps. lemon juice
- 1 tsp. dried oregano
- Salt
- Pepper

Directions:

1. Place salted water in a pot and allow to boil. Add penne. Cook pasta until firm and then drain.
2. Meanwhile, warm butter in a skillet. Add garlic and onion. Allow 2 minutes to cook.
3. Add in chicken and cook for 6 minutes, stirring occasionally. Once cooked set oven to medium-low.
4. Using a skillet, add chopped artichoke hearts, parsley, dried oregano, tomato, feta cheese, lemon juice, and drained penne pasta. Cook for approximately 3 minutes.
5. Season with salt and pepper. Serve warm.

Nutritional Information: 330 calories, 4.5g fat, 52g carbs, 20g protein

Spinach and Feta Pita Bake

Servings: 6

Ingredients:

- 6 oz. tomato pesto
- 6 whole wheat pita breads
- 2 chopped tomatoes
- 1 bunch chopped spinach
- 4 sliced mushrooms
- ½ c. crumbled feta cheese
- 2 tbsps. grated Parmesan cheese
- 3 tbsps. olive oil

Directions:

1. Set oven to 350 degrees F
2. Spread tomato pesto onto one side of each pita bread and place them pesto-side up on a baking sheet.
3. Top pitas with spinach, tomatoes, mushrooms, feta cheese, and Parmesan cheese.
4. Sprinkle with olive oil, and add pepper for seasoning.
5. Bake in preheated oven 10-12 minutes or until pitas are crisp. Cut into quarters and serve.

Nutritional Information: 350 calories, 11g protein, 17g fat, 41g carbs

Mediterranean Flounder

Servings: 4

Ingredients:

- 5 plum tomatoes
- 2 tbsps. olive oil
- ½ chopped Spanish onion
- 2 chopped garlic cloves
- 1 tsp. Italian seasoning
- 24 Kalamata olives
- ¼ c. white wine
- ¼ c. capers
- 1 tsp. fresh lemon juice
- 6 leaves of basil
- 3 tbsps. grated Parmesan cheese
- 1 lb. flounder filets
- 6 leaves basil

Directions:

1. Set oven to 425 degrees F
2. Then bring a saucepan of water to a boil. Add tomatoes and immediately remove, place in a medium bowl of ice water, then drain. Remove and discard skins from tomatoes. Chop, and then set aside.
3. In a skillet, warm olive oil. Add onion and cook until tender. Stir in tomatoes, garlic, and Italian seasoning. Cook until tomatoes are soft, 5-7 minutes.
4. Then mix in wine, capers, olives, ½ of the basil, and lemon juice. Reduce heat and stir in Parmesan cheese. Cook for approximately 15 mins. until the mixture is reduced to a thick sauce.
5. Line a shallow baking dish with your flounder filets. Pour your sauce over the filets and top with the rest of the basil.
6. Bake for about 12 minutes or until the fish is easily flaked with a fork.

Nutritional Information: 282 calories, 24g protein, 8.1g carbs, 15.4g fat

Chicken Costa Brava

Servings: 10

Ingredients:

- 20 oz. pineapple chunks
- 10 boneless chicken breast
- 1 tbsp. vegetable oil
- 1 tsp. cumin
- 1 tsp. cinnamon
- 2 minced garlic cloves
- 1 quartered onion
- 14.5 oz. stewed tomatoes
- 2 c. black olives
- ½ c. salsa
- 2 tbsps. cornstarch
- 2 tbsps. water
- 1 sliced red bell pepper
- Salt
- Pepper

Directions:

1. To begin drain the pineapple, reserving the juice. Sprinkle the chunks with salt and then set aside.
2. Next, in a large frying pan brown add oil and chicken breast. Brown the chicken breast over medium-heat. Sprinkle the chicken with cumin and cinnamon.
3. Add garlic and onion, and cook until the onion is translucent.
4. Add the reserved pineapple juice, olives, salsa, and tomatoes, cover and simmer for about 25 minutes.
5. After the mixture is finished simmering mix together the cornstarch and water. Add the cornstarch mixture to pan, as well as bell peppers. Cover and simmer until the sauce boils and thickens. Then add the pineapple chunks and heat thoroughly. Remove from heat and serve!

Nutritional Information: 239 calories, 28.6g protein, 17.6g carbs, 6.1g fat

Salmon Panzanella

Servings: 4

Ingredients:

- 8 Kalamata olives
- 3 tbsps. red wine vinegar
- 1 tbsp. capers
- ¼ tsp. ground pepper
- 3 tbsps. olive oil
- 2 slices whole-grain bread
- 2 cubed tomatoes
- 1 Medium cucumber
- ¼ c. sliced red onion
- ¼ c. sliced basil
- 1 lb. salmon
- ½ tsp. kosher salt

Directions:

1. Begin by preheating your grill to high heat.
2. Meanwhile, combine olives, vinegar, capers and 1/8 teaspoon of pepper in a large bowl. Slowly whisk in oil until thoroughly combined
3. Next, add in tomato and bread cubes, cucumber, onion, and basil. Combine completely and set aside.
4. Prepare your grill by coating it in a little bit of oil, then season both sides of the salmon with salt and pepper. Grill the salmon on both sides for 4-5 minutes each.
5. To serve divide the salad into the four portions and plate underneath the salmon.

Nutritional Information: 320 calories, 14g carbs, 18g fat, 26g protein

Stuffed Sardines

Servings: 6

Ingredients:

- ¼ c. ricotta cheese
- ¼ c. shredded Pecorino Romano cheese
- ¼ c. fresh breadcrumbs
- ¼ c. chopped parsley
- 3 large eggs
- 1 lemon
- ½ tsp. salt
- ½ tsp. ground pepper
- 12 Medium sardines
- 1/3 c. all-purpose flour
- 2 c. panko breadcrumbs
- 1 ½ c. olive oil

Directions:

1. In a medium bowl combine ricotta, Romano, parsley, fresh breadcrumbs, 1 egg, lemon zest, and ¼ teaspoon of salt and pepper. Once thoroughly combined, set aside.
2. Next, rinse the sardines and pat them dry with a paper towel. Using the remaining salt and pepper season the inside of each sardine, then stuff each with the ricotta mixture.
3. Place in three separate dishes place the 2 remaining eggs (lightly beaten), flour, and panko. Then using one hand for wet, and the other for dry dip each sardine in flour, then egg, then panko. Set sardines down on a plate and set aside.
4. Start to heat the oil in a large cast-iron skillet, over medium-high heat. You want the oil to be shimmering but not smoking. In batches of 2 fry the sardines in the oil until golden brown, approximately 2-4 minutes for each side. Serve immediately with lemon wedges!

Nutritional Information: 420 calories, 19g carbs, 26g protein, 26g fat

Desserts/Snacks

Chia Seed Pumpkin Pudding

Servings: 4

Ingredients:

- ¼ c. maple syrup
- 2 tsps. pumpkin spice
- 1 c. pumpkin puree
- 1¼ c. almond milk
- ½ c. chia seeds

Directions:

1. Soak the fixings overnight for best results or a minimum of 15 minutes.
2. Garnish with ¼ cup each of fresh blueberries, sliced almonds, and sunflower seeds.

Nutritional Information: 230 calories, 10.1g fat, 22.8g carbs, 11.7g protein

Honey Pistachio Roasted Pears

Servings: 6

Ingredients:

- 3 ripe medium pears
- 2 tbsp. butter
- 3 tbsp. honey
- ¼ c. pear nectar
- 1 tsp. grated orange zest
- 2 tbsp. powdered sugar
- ½ c. mascarpone cheese
- 1/3 c. salted pistachios

Directions:

1. Program the oven temperature to 400°F.
2. Peel, core, and cut the pears into halves. Arrange them cut side down in the baking dish.
3. Combine and add the nectar, honey, butter, and zest. Pour it over the pears. Roast with the lid off for 20-25 minutes.
4. Spoon juices over the pears occasionally and bake until tender.

Nutritional Information: 250 calories, 27g carbs, 3g protein, 15g fat

Sweet Ricotta & Strawberry Parfaits

Servings: 6

Ingredients:

- 1 lb. strawberries
- 1 tbsp. mint
- 1 tsp. sugar
- 15 oz. ricotta cheese
- 3 tbsps. light agave nectar
- ¼ tsp. shredded lemon peel
- ½ tsp. vanilla
- Fresh mint

Directions:

1. Combine the berries, sugar, and mint in a medium dish. Gently stir. Let it rest about ten minutes.
2. In another container, mix the agave nectar, ricotta, lemon peel, and vanilla. Combine with an electric mixer for two minutes using the medium speed.
3. Prepare the parfaits. Scoop one tablespoon of the mixture into each of the glasses. Top it off with the strawberry combination. Repeat the layers and garnish with the mint.
4. Serve or cover and chill for up to four hours.

Nutritional Information: 157 calories, 18g carbs, 6g fat, 9g protein

Summer Fruit Granita

Servings: 4

Ingredients:

- 1 lb. ripe nectarines
- ½ c. sugar
- ½ c. water
- ¼ c. orange juice
- 2 tbsps. lemon juice
- ½ c. raspberries

Directions:

1. Boil fruit with sugar for 10 minutes.
2. Stir in raspberries.
3. Add juice and extra sugar, if needed.
4. Let this mixture freeze for 30 minutes. Using a fork, stir ice crystals, until it's granulated.

Nutritional Information: 158 calories, 40g carbs, 0g carbs, 14g protein

Dried Figs with Ricotta & Walnuts

Servings: 4

Ingredients:

- 8 dried and halved figs
- ¼ c. ricotta cheese
- 16 halved walnut
- 1 tbsp. honey

Directions:

1. In a skillet, toast walnuts for 2 min.
2. Top figs with cheese and walnuts.
3. Drizzle with honey.

Nutritional Information: 142 calories, 4g protein, 8g fat

Banana-Strawberry Smoothie

Servings: 2

Ingredients:

- 4 tbsps. rolled oats
- ¾ c. sliced strawberries
- 1 banana
- 2 tbsps. orange juice
- 1¼ c. fat-free yogurt
- 1¼ c. skim milk
- 1 tbsp. flaxseed oil
- ¼ c. cubed ice

Directions:

1. Blend all ingredients, making a smooth mixture.

Nutritional Information: 330 calories, 5g protein, 8g fat, 48g carbs

Chocolate Mousse with Olive Oil

Servings: 6

Ingredients:

- 9½ oz. melted dark chocolate
- ⅔ c. olive oil
- 3 tbsps. orange liqueur
- 7 eggs
- ½ c. divided sugar
- Pinch of salt
- orange zest

Directions:

1. Mix the chocolate, olive oil, and liqueur in a bowl.
2. Wisk the egg yolk and half of the sugar. Combine it with chocolate mixture until smooth.
3. Stir in remaining sugar and salt.
4. Refrigerate for 20 min in small dishes before serving.

Nutritional Information: 490 calories, 8g protein, 38g fat, 30g carbs

Medjool Date Truffles

Servings: 10

Ingredients:

- 3 c. chopped Medjool dates
- 12 oz. cup brewed coffee
- 1 c. chopped pecans
- ½ c. shredded coconut
- ¾ tsp. orange zest
- 1 tsp. cinnamon, ground
- ½ c. cocoa powder

Directions:

1. Soak dates in a warm coffee for 5 minutes.
2. Remove dates from coffee and mash them, making a smooth mixture.
3. Stir in remaining ingredients except for cocoa powder.
4. Form small balls out of the mixture. Coat them with cocoa powder.

Nutritional Information: 265 calories, 43g carbs, 3g protein, 12g fat

Greek Yogurt

Servings: 2

Ingredients:

- 1 c. nonfat Greek yogurt
- 2 oranges
- 6 chopped Medjool Dates
- 2 tbsps. honey
- 2 tbsps. chopped pistachios

Directions:

1. Arrange orange slices in bowls, making semicircles.
2. Top oranges with yogurt.
3. Garnish with honey, pistachios, and dates.
4. Refrigerate for a few hours before serving.

Nutritional Information: 380 calories, 16g protein, 10g fat, 90g carbs

Peanut Butter Popcorn

Servings: 4

Ingredients:

- 2 tbsps. peanut oil
- ½ c. popcorn kernels
- ½ tsp. sea salt
- ⅓ c. chopped peanuts
- ⅓ c. peanut butter
- ¼ c. agave syrup
- ¼ c. wildflower honey

Directions:

1. Combine popcorn kernels and peanut oil in a pot.
2. Over medium heat, shake the pot gently until all corn is popped.
3. In a saucepan, combine the honey and agave syrup. Cook over low heat for 5 min, then add the peanut butter and stir.
4. Coat the popcorn with prepared sauce.

Nutritional Information: 430 calories, 9g protein, 20g fat, 56g carbs

Avocado & Blueberry Bang

Servings: 2

Ingredients:

- 1 frozen banana
- 2 quartered avocados
- 2 c. berries
- Maple syrup

Directions:

1. Blend all ingredients except agave or maple syrup. Add ice water, if needed.
2. Garnish with syrup and serve in smoothie glasses.

Nutritional Information: 250 calories, 4g protein, 13g fat, 40g carbs

Parmesan Herbed Walnuts

Servings: 8

Ingredients:

- ½ c. Parmigiano-Reggiano cheese
- ½ tsp. Italian herb seasoning
- 1 tsp. parsley flakes
- ½ tsp. garlic salt
- 2 c. walnuts
- 1 egg white
- Cayenne pepper

Directions:

1. Preheat oven to 250°F.
2. Mix all ingredients except egg white and walnuts.
3. Whisk the egg and stir in halved walnuts.
4. Combine walnuts and the cheese mixture.
5. Bake for 30 min on greased baking sheet. Serve cold.

Nutritional Information: 220 calories, 8g protein, 21g fat, 4g carbs

Figs with Blue Cheese

Servings: 2

Ingredients:

- 3 fresh figs
- 2 tbsps. blue cheese
- 1 sprig chopped rosemary
- 1½ tsps. honey

Directions:

1. Halve figs.
2. Spread cheese on each half and top with fresh rosemary. Add honey to taste.

Nutritional Information: 120 calories, 8g protein, 4g fat, 24g carbs

Evoo Cake

Servings: 8

Ingredients:

- ¾ c. olive oil
- 2 tsps. baking powder
- 1½ c. flour
- 1 c. granulated sugar
- ¼ c. milk
- 3 eggs
- Salt

Directions:

1. Set oven to 350 degrees F. Grease a cake pan.
2. Combine baking powder, flour, and ½ teaspoon salt.
3. Mix sugar and eggs, then add in olive oil and milk gradually.
4. Combine wet and dry ingredients, pour into cake pan, and bake for 40 min.

Nutritional Information: 390 calories, 5g protein, 23g fat, 45g carbs

Conclusion

Let's face it, a good diet enriched with all the nutrients is our best shot of achieving an active metabolism and an efficient lifestyle. The Mediterranean diet with all of its nourishing ingredients can make it happen. Be sure to slowly and gradually switch to the diet in order to gain its lasting impact on both mind and body. What can be more helpful is the change of approach towards your dietary habitats, only then you can fully embrace the goodness of the Mediterranean food. Treat it like a set of guidelines rather than a list of foods that are good and bad.

Thanks for reading this book. I hope this guide on the Mediterranean diet has provided you with enough insight to get you going. Don't put off getting started. The sooner you begin this diet the sooner you'll start to notice an improvement in your health and well-being. Start to care about the health of your heart immediately. While results won't come overnight, they will come if you stick to the information provided throughout this book.

Furthermore, it is my hope that you enjoy all the healthy recipes in this book. There's no shortage of meals you can enjoy on a Mediterranean diet. Having said that, the next step is to experiment with the different recipes. Enjoy the journey!

Peter Bragg

Made in the USA
Middletown, DE
03 January 2019